PAT SLOAN'S
I Can't Believe I'M Sewing!

Sewing is the best way I know to turn your dreams, your imagination, and your ideas into real life "goods." It allows you to create beautiful pieces in no time at all!

Oh, and who am I? My name is Pat Sloan, and I have an obsession with fabric. In fact, it's a life-long love affair that started with the first hand-stitched outfits I made for my dollies. It progressed to the bags, home décor, and quilts I make today. I sew to play with fabric. Simply put, I live for fabric, and after you read this book, I bet you will, too.

In these pages, you'll find the basic tools and information you need to have your sewing machine humming and the needle moving lickety-split. You'll not only learn how to sew, but how to get sewing **fast** and **furious**! Once you get the bug, all you'll want to do is make stuff. I know, I've been there—still am. So take my hand and let's get going!

LEISURE ARTS, INC.
Little Rock, Arkansas

TABLE OF Contents

Pat Sloan's "I Can't Believe I'm Sewing!"

SEWING MACHINE Features

So, you've got the sewing "bug." What kind of machine do you need? What features does it need to complete the projects you want to make? Do you have to invest a lot of money? The great projects in this book require a very basic sewing machine. All the "bells and whistles" are not necessary. The following features are all you need in the beginning:

A Straight Stitch
All machines will have this. Most machines will have a button that when engaged allows the machine to stitch backwards or backstitch. This is used to secure the ends of your stitching lines.

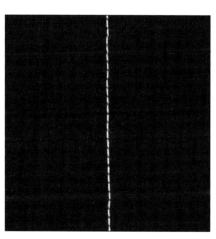

Bobbins
These hold the lower thread. Be sure you have the **CORRECT** bobbins for your machine.

A Zigzag Stitch
Almost all machines will have this. You may find a very old machine or a very inexpensive new machine that only does a straight stitch.

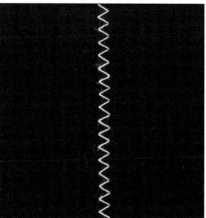

A Manual
If you are gifted with a machine with no manual, check the internet or check with your local sewing machine dealer to see if they can order a manual for you.

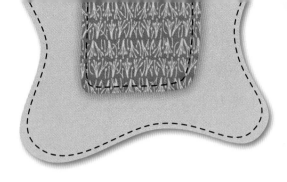

In order to get sewing quickly you will need a sewing machine. But first...HOW do you get a machine if you don't have one? Try these simple ways to bring a sewing machine into your life:

- Ask your family, co-workers, neighbors, and friends if they have a machine they can either loan you or give you.

- Check out flea markets, yard sales, and thrift stores.

- Put a notice up on church, library, and grocery store bulletin boards asking if anyone has an old machine for sale.

- Visit your local sewing machine dealer for a used machine that has been fully serviced.

- For a new machine, check out your local sewing machine dealer. Also, there are nice little starter machines available at department stores. These are not fancy machines, but will get you doing the basics on a new machine for a small price.

Now that you have a machine, lets's have some fun! Without thread and without fabric...just plug in the "gas pedal" and push it. See how fast the machine runs. Push it a little...then put the "pedal to the metal." You can't break anything. Just get a feel for how it works!

To get started, refer to your sewing machine manual to wind and insert a bobbin and to thread your machine. If you don't have a manual, refer to pages 46-48 for the basics of preparing your machine for sewing. Depending on the age and last time your machine was used, it may need to be cleaned and oiled. To learn how to maintain your machine, refer to your manual or turn to page 49.

Pat Sloan's "I Can't Believe I'm Sewing!"

Parts of the Machine

This photo shows different parts of a sewing machine. While the parts of a machine are generally all the same, your sewing machine manual will show you the location of all the parts of *your* machine.

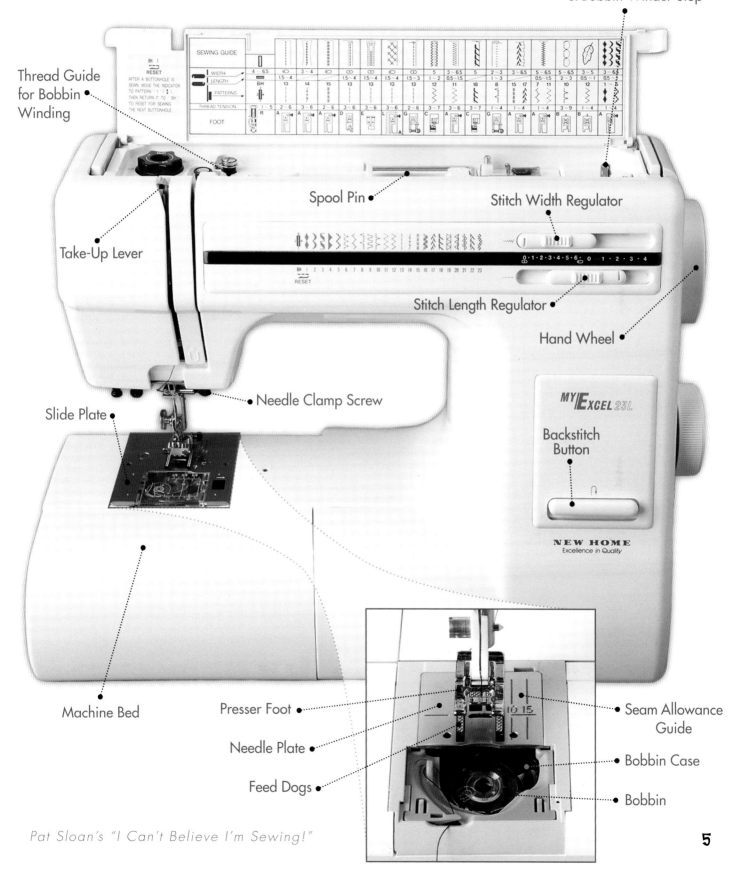

Bobbin Winder Spindle & Bobbin Winder Stop

Thread Guide for Bobbin Winding

Take-Up Lever

Spool Pin

Stitch Width Regulator

Stitch Length Regulator

Hand Wheel

Needle Clamp Screw

Slide Plate

Backstitch Button

Machine Bed

Presser Foot

Needle Plate

Feed Dogs

Seam Allowance Guide

Bobbin Case

Bobbin

MY EXCEL 23L

NEW HOME
Excellence in Quality

Pat Sloan's "I Can't Believe I'm Sewing!"

SeWiNg

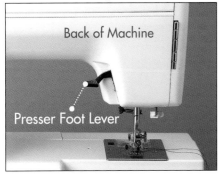

Fig. 1

Give Her A Test Drive!

Cut two 4" x 8" strips of cotton fabric. Matching right sides and raw edges, place the two fabric pieces together and pin. Do **NOT** put pins where you will sew. You never want to sew over a pin because a pin jammed into the bobbin case is **NOT** a good thing.

Refer to Fig. 1 to raise the presser foot (found on the back or left end of the machine). Place your fabric **UNDER** the presser foot. Lower the presser foot lever so the foot is now flat on the throat plate.

Press the "gas pedal" and start the machine running. The little feed dog "teeth" under the presser foot will start going up and down. Those feed dogs will pull the fabric under the presser foot. You don't need to push it, just guide it.

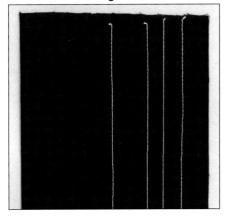

Fig. 2

Sew a line the length of the fabrics and stop; cut thread. Sew additional lines (**Fig. 2**) and try running the "gas pedal" faster and slower to get a feel for how it runs.

Checking The Stitch

At this point, check the stitch to see if the tension is correct. This is **SUPER** important as you don't want your project falling apart or being all puckered up!

Your stitches should be smooth and have an even tension on top and bottom and pretty much look the same from both sides (Fig. 3).

Fig. 3

Your machine has a tension control knob or dial (Fig. 4). This is used to adjust the tension on the top thread. Adjusting the tension will help you achieve a beautiful stitch.

If the tension is too tight, the fabric will pucker and you will see the bobbin thread pulled up to the top side. If this is the case, change the dial to a lower number.

If the tension is too loose, the bobbin thread will make loose loops and the top thread will just "lay" on the surface. In this case, change the dial to a higher number.

Adjust the tension one full number and sew another test. If it has gone too far, adjust back half a number. Continue until the stitch looks good.

Sewing Machine Feet

You should have a "standard" foot that looks something like this (Fig. 5). This foot is used most often for straight stitching and zigzag stitching. Loosen the thumbscrew at the top of the foot, slide the current foot off, and slide the standard foot on. Tighten the screw. Some feet simply have a slot and "pop" on and off with a gentle tug or by pressing a release button.

Seam Allowance

What IS a seam allowance? When sewing, it's the area from the needle or stitching line to the edge of the fabric.

Always sew with the bulk of the fabric to the left of the needle. If your needle position can be changed, place your needle in the center position. Your sewing machine has lines and possibly measurements etched into the throat plate (Fig. 6). These lines indicate the distance from the needle to the edge of the fabric. Line up the edge of the fabric on a line of the throat plate. That is your guide.

Seam allowance width will vary with the project you are completing. Refer to your project instructions to determine the correct seam allowance for your project. Garment construction usually uses a ⅝" seam allowance, sewing home décor usually uses a ½" seam allowance, and quilt piecing usually uses a ¼" seam allowance (Fig. 7).

Why do you care? You care because patterns are drawn and measurements are given **INCLUDING** the seam allowance. If you sew with too much or too little seam allowance, then the pieces won't fit together. Consistent seam allowance width is very important. It's math, science, and magic all rolled into one! Joking aside, it's like a puzzle.

Fig. 4

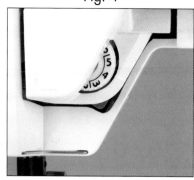

Fig. 5

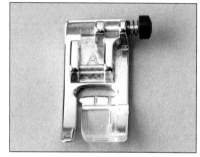

Fig. 6

Fig. 7

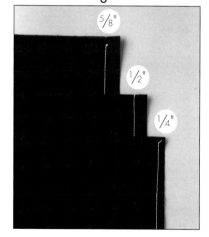

Stitch Length

The average stitch length is 2.5 to 3 mm or approximately 12 stitches per inch. So the straight stitch setting on your machine should be at 2.5 or 3 or at 12 stitches per inch. Some machines even automatically adjust to that setting when turned on.

Foot Control

Fig. 8

The foot control (Fig. 8) is just like the gas pedal of a car. Zoom, zoom! Be sure it is plugged into the sewing machine. Sounds basic, but things happen!

Backstitching

To lock the stitch in place at beginning of seams, sew forward about 2 or 3 stitches. Then push your "backwards" button on the machine and sew backwards for 2 or 3 stitches. This locks your stitches so they don't come out. This is also done at the end of seams.

Pinning the project

Fig. 9

Straight pins are used to pin fabric layers together for sewing. This prevents the layers from slipping and keeps the edges together securely.

I pin with the head on the **OUTSIDE**, perpendicular to the edge I'll be sewing (Fig. 9). That way I can easily remove the pin before I sew over it. **DON'T** sew over a pin! If you hit it many bad things can happen. The worst being it bends down into the bobbin case and damages it.

Visit **LeisureArts.com** to see Pat's webcasts on sewing machine and rotary cutting basics. You'll find them under **Quilting** on the webcasts page!

Pat Sloan's "I Can't Believe I'm Sewing!"

LET'S TALK Fabric

Fabric, material...the good stuff in life! There are many types of fabrics. Just look at what your clothing, furniture, linens, and coats are made of. There is lightweight, medium-weight and heavyweight.

For these projects I recommend cotton, cotton blend, linen, or denim. I feel the easiest fabric to learn to sew with is cotton or a cotton blend. These fabrics aren't slippery and are lightweight so you don't have thickness or bulk to deal with. They are easy to find, and they come in a zillion beautiful patterns and colors.

So...Where DO You Find Fabric?

There are fabric and fabric/craft stores in many neighborhoods. Look in your phone book under Fabric. (But I'll bet you've found them all already!)

♦ You can do that "asking around" again. Many of your friends, family, co-workers and neighbors have fabric they have never used (this is called a "stash").

♦ Thrift shops and yard sales have fabric.

♦ Visit home decorator stores (where they sell fabric for curtains and upholstery). Check the sale tables for good deals on ends and returns.

♦ Clothing – ahhhh...a special category of its own. Recycled clothing **CAN** be remade into many smaller projects if you wash it first and avoid using any stained areas.

For now, when using clothing, look for mostly cotton shirts and skirts. Denim fabric from an old pair of jeans is awesome because it has weight. But the fabric is usually not that wide. Blazers or jackets usually have too much inner construction to work with. But you never know!

♦ Linens, such as tablecloths, tea towels, curtains, and even a coverlet can be reused.

♦ On-line – the internet is a great source for both old and new fabrics.

How To Pick Fabric For Your Projects

♦ Feel – The weight and "drape factor" of the fabric should fit the project you are doing. For a project that needs to "drape", like a curtain, you want fabric that will flow when you hang it. Take the fabric and hold it up and see how it hangs. If it is stiff, then pick another fabric. You may not like the feel for curtains but it might work great for a tote bag.

♦ Color – This is the **BEST** part of sewing… picking the colors and designs. This is **WHY** I sew. My color tips:

Pick a color theme and style, such as, French Country with its yellows and blues, Cottage-Style with creams, aquas and browns, or Craftsman-Style of browns, greens and rusts. Maybe Bohemian in deep jewel tones of purples, golds and moss green are your favorite.

Go shopping! Find fabrics in your color theme and style. Lay the fabrics out next to each other. Mix up the print sizes so you have large, medium, and small prints.

If you only chose a few fabrics, then select prints that complement each other by either blending together or having contrast.

As you look at the projects in the book, note the fabrics used. If the project is not in a color or fabric choice you like, don't throw out the project. Select some fabrics that suit you and audition them for the project. Try out several combinations.

♦ Fabric Grain – Because fabric is woven on a loom, some threads go along the length and some threads go across the width of the fabric.

Along the lengthwise edges are the selvages. These edges of the fabric are very dense and have largish holes and often one selvage has writing. You don't want to use the selvages because they are very tightly woven and usually stretch very little.

The threads going lengthwise and parallel to the selvages (Fig. 1) are the least stretchy direction of the fabric.

Fig. 1

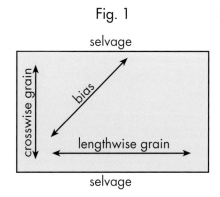

The threads going crosswise and perpendicular to the selvages (Fig. 1) are the second least stretchy direction.

Bias is the direction along the 45° angle on the fabric (Fig. 1). It has the most stretch.

Project pieces with the edges cut parallel to either straight grain (lengthwise or crosswise) are less likely to stretch out of shape than pieces with edges cut along the bias, because the interwoven threads give the cut edges extra support.

The project pattern will let you know if you need to cut out the pattern pieces using any special grain requirements. Pattern pieces may have a grainline arrow. This is a black line with arrows on each end. This symbol means to pin the pattern to the fabric so that this arrow is aligned with the lengthwise grain of the fabric.

So why do you need to know this? Sometimes it helps your project to have the fabric stretch a lot or not at all. When you have those requirements your project turns out better when it is placed on the best direction on the fabric. For example, a twirly skirt usually needs to have lots of bias edge at the hem so you have the best drape. Or, a long border on a bedspread will lay nice and flat when cut on the least stretchy length of the fabric.

Pre-Washing Fabric

To wash or not to wash, that is the question! I'll give you the background, then you decide!

Why It's Good To Pre-wash

♦ Fabrics have chemicals on them used in the printing process. It is good to wash them out, as some people are sensitive.

♦ Fabrics might have extra dyes that will "bleed" out when washed. If you do not pre-wash the fabrics, when you wash the finished item, one or more fabrics may release dyes and stain the project.

♦ Washing softens the feel of the fabric. If a fabric is going to change in the way it feels with washing, you want to know that ahead of time and not have a problem project later. Pre-washing is nice for home decor fabrics as they can be stiff with repellents and finishes that you may not want.

♦ Some fabrics shrink a bit. So if you pre-wash, the fabric is at its final size **BEFORE** you cut out the pattern — a good thing. If you do not pre-wash and you make and launder a shower curtain, the length may not be as long as you wish. Or, if you make a garment, the finished garment may not fit properly after it's washed.

Why It's Good To Not Pre-wash

♦ Unwashed fabric will keep it's color and crispness. If you never intend to wash the project, then you may want to skip pre-washing.

♦ When you wash the fabric it often becomes more limp. You can correct this by spray starching pieces that are too limp to work with.

♦ If the fabric has sheen on it (such as a polished cotton), washing usually removes that sheen.

LET'S TALK Thread

There are many types of thread in the store, but don't let the huge selection overwhelm you. Most of the fancy threads you'll see are for decorative work such as embroidery machines, machine quilting, and fancy embellishment work.

For regular sewing on cotton, upholstery, and jeans fabric (non-stretchy material) it is easy to find thread. You can use most "General Purpose" sewing threads. They will be one of the following:

♦ Cotton
♦ Cotton-wrapped Polyester
♦ Polyester

Thread also has a weight. The LARGER the number the THINNER the thread...hmmm... wish that worked with my weight!!

You want to use a 50 weight thread for general purpose sewing. The number will be on the side or top of the spool...50 wt.

I highly recommend you try a name brand thread. Many of the less expensive and no name threads will break easier and have a lot of thread dust that creates more lint buildup. Remember, thread might not be that exciting, but it holds all your work together. Just like putting cheap tires on the car...it's not a good idea. Cheap thread isn't either. You want your work to last.

Most machines are happiest when the top and bobbin thread are the same. You **CAN** use different threads, but then you have to adjust your tension.

To determine the thread color to use you have 2 things to consider.
♦ Are you sewing seams that won't be seen? If so, pick a neutral color like off-white, grey, tan, brown, or black. Use light color thread for light fabrics. Use dark color thread for dark fabrics.

♦ Are you topstitching where your thread will be seen? If so, you want a thread color that blends (at least until you feel comfy with your sewing). To know if the thread color "blends", do the following:

The thread on the spool is much darker than it will be as a single strand. So you really need to view it as one strand. Take a piece of the fabric you're using over to the thread rack. If possible, unwind the thread a bit and lay one strand on the fabric. Pick a color that blends or is a shade darker. I suggest darker because light comes "toward" you and dark "recedes" from view.

Note: Some spools have the thread end glued under the paper on top of the spool. In this case, do your best to pick a thread from the spool color but go lighter than you think as it reads darker when it's wound around the spool.

LET'S TALK Notions

There are many, many notions made to make your sewing faster and more enjoyable. Here are a few of the necessities:

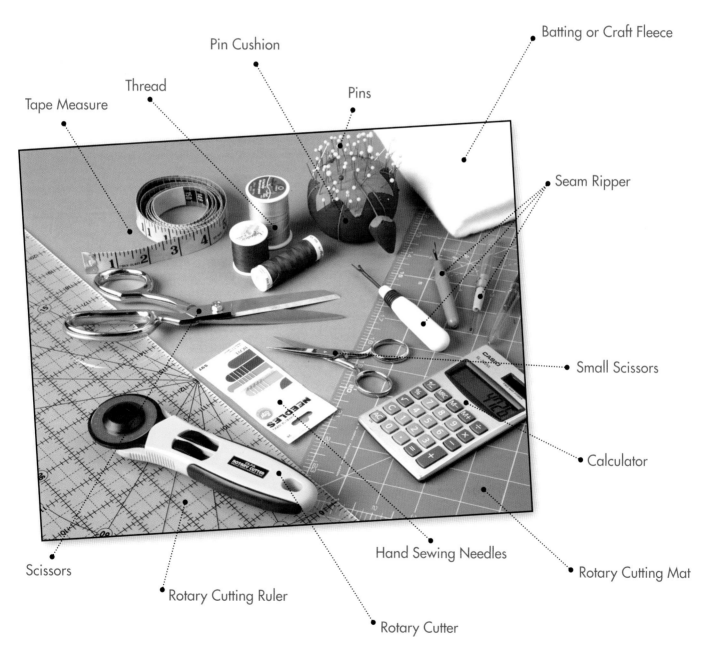

Batting or Craft Fleece

Pin Cushion

Thread

Pins

Tape Measure

Seam Ripper

Small Scissors

Calculator

Scissors

Hand Sewing Needles

Rotary Cutting Ruler

Rotary Cutting Mat

Rotary Cutter

LET'S MAKE OUR FIRST PROJECT –
A Coaster Set

My first simple project is a coaster set. This will allow you to get your creative juices flowing and it will show you how very easy and fast it is to make something.

Supplies

The measurements given are adequate for making 4 coasters.

♦ 6" x 22" (15 cm x 56 cm) piece of 100% cotton fabric - Look around for something approximately this size to practice with. Fabric from the bolt is approximately 40" wide. If you don't have a scrap this size, buy ¼ yard - that's 9". Keep with cotton, if possible. It's easier to practice on.

♦ 6" x 22" (15 cm x 56 cm) piece of a heavier 100% cotton fabric - It would be great if this piece had more weight than the other fabric. It can be denim fabric from an old pair of jeans, an old tea towel, or a lightweight canvas-type fabric.

♦ Optional: 6" x 22" (15 cm x 56 cm) piece of batting - to give the piece some weight

♦ 100% cotton thread or a poly-wrapped cotton thread.

♦ A chopstick for turning and pushing out the corners. (Oh! Good time to order carryout!)

Cutting Out The Pieces

Included in this book is a drawing of a 5" x 5" square (page 17). This is your "pattern" for this project. Photocopy the page and cut out the pattern.

Place the pattern on the wrong side of the fabric and draw around the pattern (Fig. 1). Cut out the fabric piece along the drawn line with your scissors.

From cotton fabric (top fabric):
  ♦ Cut 4 squares 5" x 5".
From heavier fabric (back fabric):
  ♦ Cut 4 squares 5" x 5".
From batting (optional):
  ♦ Cut 4 squares 5" x 5".

Making The Coasters

Match right sides and raw edges and use a ¼" seam allowance throughout. Refer to **Pressing***, page 51.*

1. Lay a top square and a bottom square together with the "good" or "right" sides facing each other and the raw edges even. (If you don't have a heavy fabric on the back, place the batting square on top of the fabric squares.) Pin the edges of the squares together.

Tip: Fabric has a bit of a mind of it's own. It has some stretch, so you want to handle it gently when sewing and pressing. You don't want to stretch it so it's longer...just hold it in place as you work and all will be fine!

2. Using a ¼" seam allowance and beginning about 2" from one corner, backstitch. As you sew, remove the pins before you sew over them.

Fig. 1

3. Sew to ¼" from the next corner. (If you like you can make a pencil dot, or place a pin there. When you reach that point, turn the hand wheel to put your needle **DOWN** into the fabric (Fig. 2).

4. Lift the presser foot and pivot the squares. You should now be ready to sew the next edge with a ¼" seam allowance.

5. Repeat Steps 3-4 to sew sides 3 and 4.

6. Now you are back on side 1 where you started. Sew about 1" and backstitch, leaving an opening for turning (Fig. 3).

7. Lift the presser foot and pull the squares out to the side. Cut the threads, leaving short thread tails.

8. Trim the corners so there is less bulk (Fig. 4). They will look nicer when turned and pressed.

Fig. 2

Fig. 3

Fig. 4

Pat Sloan's "I Can't Believe I'm Sewing!"

9. Turn the coaster through the opening (like you were turning a bed pillowcase) so the "good" or "right" sides of the fabrics are outside and your raw edges are inside (Fig. 5). Use your chopstick to carefully push all 4 corners out (Fig. 6).

10. Press the coaster flat. As you do this, press the opening seam allowances to the **INSIDE**.

11. To close the opening and make a nice edge, edgestitch around the coaster (Fig. 7). This means sewing very close to the edge. Starting on the middle of one side, do a backstitch to lock the threads. Sew all the way around. End where you started and do another backstitch.

12. Lift the presser foot and trim the threads right next to the fabric so there are no tails.

Fig. 5

Fig. 6

Fig. 7

Coaster Pattern

Photocopy pattern or trace pattern onto paper. Cut out pattern along drawn line. Place pattern on fabric and draw around pattern. Cut out along drawn line.

Guess what?
You just finished your first project! Now make the rest of the coasters. Wasn't that **FAST** and **FUN**!

THE PERFECT Table Runner

These table runners are the perfect way to get to know your sewing machine. Just use 1 fabric for the table runner top shown on page 19. Or, be a little adventurous and use 2 fabrics for the table runner top shown at left. Easy projects, fabulous results...a winner every time!

Supplies
Yardage is based on 43"/44" (109 cm/112 cm) wide fabric.

For 1-fabric runner
½ yd (46 cm) of fabric for table runner top
1⅜ yds (1.3 m) of fabric for table runner back
20" x 44" (51 cm x 112 cm) piece of thin batting (optional)

For 2-fabric runner
½ yd (46 cm) of fabric for table runner top center
¼ yd (23 cm) of fabric for table runner top ends
1⅜ yds (1.3 m) of fabric for table runner back
20" x 44" (51 cm x 112 cm) piece of thin batting (optional)

More About Backing Fabric
Many fabrics you might select for the top of the runner are lightweight and have a soft drape. Putting two of those fabrics together doesn't make a very "firm" runner. For a firmer runner you can use a "filler" such as cotton quilt batting or craft fleece along with the table runner back. If you don't want a "filler" then I suggest using denim, firm muslin, heavier linen, or upholstery fabric for your table runner back.

Tips:
♦ Select a fabric that goes with your decor.

♦ Select a fabric that has a theme...such as spring flowers or fall leaves.

♦ Make the project as a gift — for a baby shower (use to decorate the baby's dresser)...for Mother's Day...for a new neighbor...add a few coasters and put them in a really cute gift bag! This is such a personal gift and people will be thrilled!

♦ Don't want such a long runner? Just measure the length you would like your table runner and cut your fabric that length plus ½".

Cutting Out The Pieces

All measurements include ¼" seam allowances.

From table runner top fabric(s):

♦ Cut **table runner top** 16" x 40" *or* if using 2 fabrics, cut **table runner top center** 16" x 25" and 2 **table runner top ends** 16" x 8".

From table runner back fabric:

♦ Cut **table runner back** 20" x 44".

Making The Table Runner

Match right sides and raw edges and use a ¼" seam allowance throughout. Refer to Pressing, page 51.

1. For 2-fabric table runner top, sew one long edge of one table runner top end to each short edge of the table runner top center.

2. Place backing fabric, right side up, on work surface. With right side down, center the table runner top (1-fabric or 2-fabric) on the backing fabric. There will be a little backing fabric showing around all the edges of the table runner top. This is easier than cutting them the same size.
   Note: If the backing is shifting as you try to layer the pieces you may want to use painter's tape to tape the backing to the table.

3. If a "filler" is desired, place the batting on top of the table runner top.

4. Pin all layers together.

5. You are going to make this just like the coasters. Leaving about a 10" opening for turning, sew around all sides of table runner top.

Tip: When sewing through all these layers, use a walking foot on your sewing machine. The walking foot will pull the layers evenly through the machine.

6. Trim the backing and batting (if used) even with the top. Turn the runner right side out, pushing out the 4 corners; press well.

7. To close the opening and make a nice edge, edgestitch around the runner close to the edge.

SCARF Magic

Approximate Finished Size:
4" x 39½" (10 cm x 100 cm)

With a few basics you can create a multitude of different scarves. The fabric and embellishments change the look entirely!

Tips:

♦ I used fleece for the back of this scarf and for the flowers. Fleece comes in many thicknesses…I suggest a thin fleece, as it's easier to sew and makes a less bulky scarf.

♦ You can add more flowers to your scarf if you like…I think a scarf full of flowers would be awesome!

♦ The front fabric I used is a stripe that worked really well to give a pieced look (without the work) to this scarf.

♦ If you use cotton fabric instead of fleece for the flowers and flower centers the edges will fray more than the fleece. I like that look!

♦ This scarf would be great using a Christmas fabric or a novelty print like little snowmen or ice skates! Maybe even your favorite sports team logos…good for a "guy gift" too.

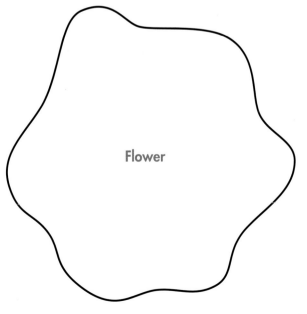

Flower

Photocopy patterns or trace patterns onto paper. Cut out patterns along drawn line. Place patterns on fabric and draw around patterns. Cut out along drawn line.

Flower Center

Supplies

Yardage is based on 43"/44"
(109 cm/112 cm) wide cotton fabric and
58"/60" (147 cm/152 cm) fleece fabric.

¼ yd (23 cm) of cotton fabric for top
¼ yd (23 cm) of fleece fabric for back
Assorted scraps of fleece for flowers
3 assorted buttons

Cutting Out The Pieces

All measurements include ¼" seam
allowances.

From cotton fabric:
- ♦ Cut **top** 4½" x 40".

From fleece fabric:
- ♦ Cut **back** 4½" x 40".

From assorted scraps of fleece fabric:
- ♦ Use patterns, page 20, to cut
  3 **flowers** and 3 **flower centers**.

Making The Scarf

Match right sides and raw edges and use a
¼" seam allowance throughout. I recommend
using a walking foot when sewing. Refer to
Pressing, page 51.

1. Starting on one long side, sew
   top and back together, leaving a
   5" opening for turning.

2. Turn scarf right side out, pushing out the
   corners. Press well so the edges are flat.

3. To close the opening and make a nice
   edge, topstitch ¼" from the outside
   edges of the scarf.

4. Pin **flowers** and **flower centers** on one
   end of scarf. Sew in a circle to secure
   flowers and centers to scarf.

5. Sew a button in the center of each
   flower by hand.

6. After stitching, I "rolled" up the edges
   of each flower to give them dimension.

Pat Sloan's "I Can't Believe I'm Sewing!"

There are SO MANY cute baby fabrics available. Look in fabric stores or buy cute sheets…either will work! I used a Mother Goose print for the green border on one of the blankets, page 25, and a funky bird print for the other blanket, page 23. Both prints will work for either boys or girls!

· ·

Supplies

Yardage is based on 43"/44" (109 cm/112 cm) wide cotton fabric and 58"/60" (147 cm/152 cm) wide Minkee or fleece.

⅝ yd (57 cm) of fabric #1 for squares
⅜ yd (34 cm) of fabric #2 for squares
⅜ yd (34 cm) of fabric for inner border
1⅜ yds (1.3 m) of fabric for outer border
1½ yds (1.4 m) of a soft fabric such as Minkee or fleece for backing

Cutting Out The Pieces

All measurements include ¼" seam allowances.
From fabric #1:
  ♦ Cut 5 **squares** 8½" x 8½".
From fabric #2:
  ♦ Cut 4 **squares** 8½" x 8½".
From inner border fabric:
  ♦ Cut 2 *crosswise* **top/bottom inner borders** 2½" x 24½".
  ♦ Cut 2 *crosswise* **side inner borders** 2½" x 28½".

From outer border fabric:
  ♦ Cut 2 *lengthwise* **top/bottom outer borders** 7½" x 28½".
  ♦ Cut 2 *lengthwise* **side outer borders** 7½" x 42½".
From fabric for backing:
  ♦ Cut **backing square** 46½" x 46½".

Making The Baby Blanket

Refer to **Blanket Top Diagram**, *page 24. Match right sides and raw edges and use a ¼" seam allowance throughout. Refer to* **Pressing**, *page 51.*

1. Sew one fabric #1 **square** on opposite sides of a fabric #2 **square** to make **Row A**. Make 2 Row A's.

Row A (make 2)

2. Sew one fabric #2 **square** on opposite sides of a fabric #1 **square** to make Row B.

Row B

3. Sew Row A's and Row B together to make blanket top center.

4. Sew **top** and **bottom inner borders** to blanket top center.

5. Sew **side inner borders** to sides of blanket top.

6. Sew **top** and **bottom outer borders** to blanket top.

7. Sew **side outer borders** to sides of blanket top.

8. Lay **backing square**, right side up, on a table. Clamp or tape backing to table along two opposite sides (**Fig. 1**).

Fig. 1

9. Center the top, right side down, on the backing square.

10. Using safety pins, pin ½" from the outside edges of the top (**Fig. 2**). With the pins ½" away from the edge you can sew without removing the safety pins. When you have pinned all the edges, shift the whole thing to pin the rest.

Fig. 2

11. Place 2 or 3 safety pins in the center area to secure it so it won't shift and it will be easier to handle.

Tip: Use the walking foot on your sewing machine. The fleece is thicker than cotton and the walking foot will pull the layers evenly through the machine.

12. Sew around all edges, leaving about a 10" opening for turning. Trim the batting even with the top. Remove the safety pins and turn the blanket right side out, being sure to push out the corners. Press well so the edges are flat.

13. To close the opening and make a nice edge, edgestitch around the outside of the blanket close to the edge.

14. Stitch in the ditch along each side of the inner border and around each block.

Blanket Top Diagram

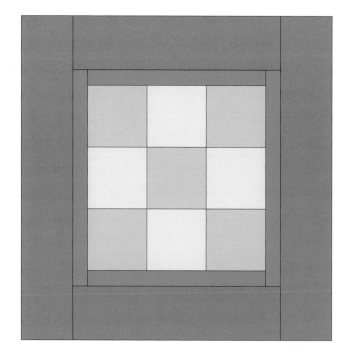

Pat Sloan's "I Can't Believe I'm Sewing!"

A "GREEN" Grocery Sack

Finished Size:
16" x 18¼" (41 cm x 46 cm)

Basic Sack
(Shown on far right in photo, page 27.)

Supplies
Yardage is based on 43"/44" (109 cm/112 cm) wide fabric.

- ⅝ yd (57 cm) of fabric for sack body
- ⅝ yd (57 cm) of fabric for sack lining
- ¼ yd (23 cm) of fabric for handles
- Two 1½" x 23" (4 cm x 58 cm) strips of batting (a thin batting works best)
- Buttons – four 1⅜" (35 mm) and four 1⅛" (29 mm)

Cutting Out The Pieces
All measurements include ¼" seam allowances.
From fabric for sack body:
- ◆ Cut 1 **sack body** 16½" x 36½".

From sack lining fabric:
- ◆ Cut 1 **sack lining** 16½" x 38½".

From handle fabric:
- ◆ Cut 2 **handles** 4" x 24".

Making The Grocery Sack
*Match right sides and raw edges and use a ¼" seam allowance throughout. Refer to **Pressing**, page 51.*

1. For body of sack, match right sides and short ends to fold **sack body** in half so that it is 16½" x 18¼".
2. For side seams, sew long edges together. Turn right side out and press.
3. Repeat **Steps 1-2** with **sack lining** so that it is 16½" x 19¼" before turning.
4. Press the top edge of the sack lining ¼" to the wrong side. Press the pressed top edge ¾" to the wrong side.
5. Place the sack lining **inside** the sack body.
6. Slip the top edge of the sack body **under** the folded edge of the sack lining; pin.

Tip: Put your walking foot on the machine to make it easier to sew the bulk.

7. Edgestitch along the bottom fold of the sack lining to secure the 2 pieces together. Edgestitch a second time along the top edge.
8. For handle, press each edge of **handle** ½" to the wrong side.
9. Place the batting strip on the wrong side of the handle, slipping 1 long edge and short edges under the folds of the handle.
10. Fold the remaining side of handle over the batting so the two long folded edges are aligned. Edgestitch folded edges of the handle.
11. Set your machine to a **wide** zigzag stitch. Zigzag down the middle of the handle.
12. Refer to Fig. 1 to position the center of each end of one handle 4" from each side seam; pin in place inside the bag.

Fig. 1

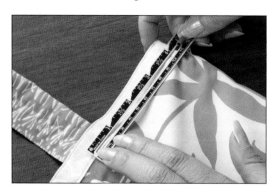

Pat Sloan's "I Can't Believe I'm Sewing!"

13. Refer to Fig. 2 to topstitch each end of handle in place.

Fig. 2

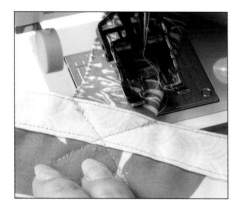

14. Repeat **Steps 8-13** to attach remaining handle.
15. Sew two stacked buttons on each end of the handle over the stitching and **GO SHOPPING**!

Sack With Contrasting Bottom

Supplies
Yardage is based on 43"/44" (109 cm/112 cm) wide fabric.
   ½ yd (46 cm) of fabric for sack body
   ⅝ yd (57 cm) of fabric for sack lining
   ½ yd (46 cm) of fabric for sack bottom and handles
   ⅛ yd (11 cm) of fabric for accent strip
   Two 1½" x 23" (4 cm x 58 cm) strips of batting (a thin batting works best)
   Buttons – four 1½" (38 mm) and four smaller

Cutting Out The Pieces
All measurements include ¼" seam allowances.
From fabric for sack body:
   ♦ Cut 2 **sack bodies** 16½" x 12½".
From sack lining fabric:
   ♦ Cut **sack lining** 16½" x 38½".
From fabric for sack bottom and handles:
   ♦ Cut 2 **sack bottoms** 16½" x 5".
   ♦ Cut 2 **handles** 4" x 24".
From accent fabric:
   ♦ Cut 2 **accent strips** 16½" x 1½".

Making The Grocery Sack
*Match right sides and raw edges and use a ¼" seam allowance throughout. Refer to **Pressing**, page 51.*
1. For sack front, refer to Fig. 1 to sew 1 **sack body**, 1 **accent strip**, and 1 **sack bottom** together. Repeat for sack back.

Fig. 1

2. Sew sack front and back together along 2 long edges and 1 short edge.
3. For sack lining, match right sides and fold the **sack lining** in half so that it is 16½" x 19¼". For side seams, sew long edges together. Turn right side out and press.
4. Follow **Basic Sack**, Steps 4-15 to complete grocery sack.

A "DITTY BAG" For Every Use

Approximate Finished Size:
10" x 10½" (25 cm x 27 cm)

My original little "Ditty Bag" was made to hold clothespins. I needed something to "pin" to the clothesline when I was hanging laundry. It reminds me of the clothespin bag my grandmother used when she hung the laundry out.

Since making my first Ditty Bag I have used them for SO much more! Fill one with goodies for kids or girlfriends. Make a fancy bag in velvet or use some nice home decor fabric you have left from a project. Hang it on a doorknob and fill it with items you need to remember to take with you, like sunglasses or letters to mail. They tuck inside bigger bags ever so nicely.

They don't take much fabric, so they are great for using up smaller pieces. Ever so useful, the ditty bag will become your "go to" project!

Supplies

Yardage is based on 43"/44" (109 cm/112 cm) wide fabric.
   13" x 26" (33 cm x 66 cm) rectangle of outer fabric
   ½ yd (46 cm) of lining fabric
   Scraps of assorted fabrics for embellishment (optional)

Cutting The Pieces

All measurements include ¼" seam allowances. Use patterns, page 32.
From outer fabric:
   ♦ Cut 2 **ditty bags**.
From lining fabric:
   ♦ Cut 2 **ditty bags**.
   ♦ Cut 2 **strap casings** 2" x 7".
   ♦ Cut 2 **straps** 2" x 20".
From two different embellishment fabrics (optional):
   ♦ Cut 1 **large circle**.
   ♦ Cut 1 **small circle**.

Making The Bag

*Match right sides and raw edges and use a ¼" seam allowance throughout. Refer to **Pressing**, page 51.*

1. For bag front, sew 1 outer fabric **ditty bag** and 1 lining fabric **ditty bag** together (**Fig. 1**), leaving a 3" opening at the bottom for turning. Turn right side out; press. Edgestitch close to edge around entire front.

Fig. 1

2. For bag back, repeat **Step 1** using remaining **ditty bag** pieces.
3. Press all edges of each **strap casing** ¼" to the wrong side.
4. On the lining side of the ditty bag front, center the strap casing, right side up, 2½" below the top edge; pin.
5. Backstitching at beginning and end of stitching, stitch strap casing to lining side of bag front along long edges.
6. Repeat **Steps 4 & 5** using remaining strap casing and bag back.
7. If adding embellishment, place **small circle** in center of **large circle**; pin circles to ditty bag. Stitch circles to bag in a circular pattern (**Fig. 2**).

Fig. 2

8. Place bag front and bag back together. Starting and stopping at the bottom of the strap casing, topstitch ⅛" inside the previous edgestitching around sides and bottom. This gives a nice double stitch look on the lower edge.
9. Press all edges of each **strap** ¼" to the wrong side.
10. Matching wrong sides, press strap in half lengthwise. Using steam in your iron will make a nice crease. Edgestitch along all sides.
11. Repeat **Step 10** for the remaining strap.
12. Pin a safety pin to one end of strap (**Fig. 3**). Thread it through the strap casing on bag front (**Fig. 4**). Repeat to thread remaining strap through casing on bag back.

Fig. 3

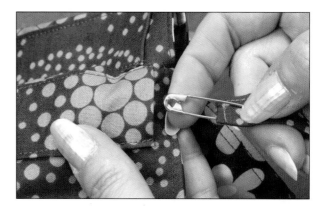

Fig. 4

13. Knot the ends together on each side of bag in a simple overhand knot.

Fill and enjoy!

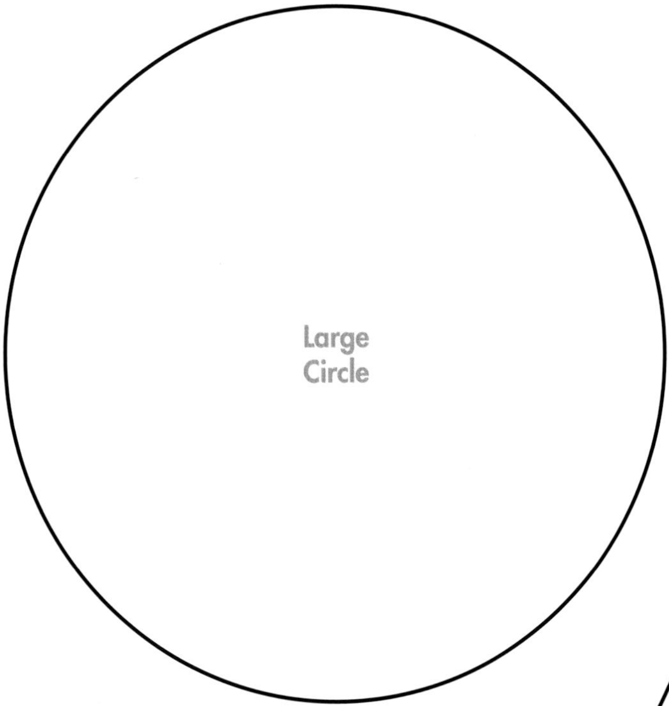

**Large
Circle**

*Photocopy circle patterns or
trace patterns onto paper.
Cut out patterns along line.
Place patterns on fabric and
draw around pattern. Cut out
along drawn line.*

Ditty Bag

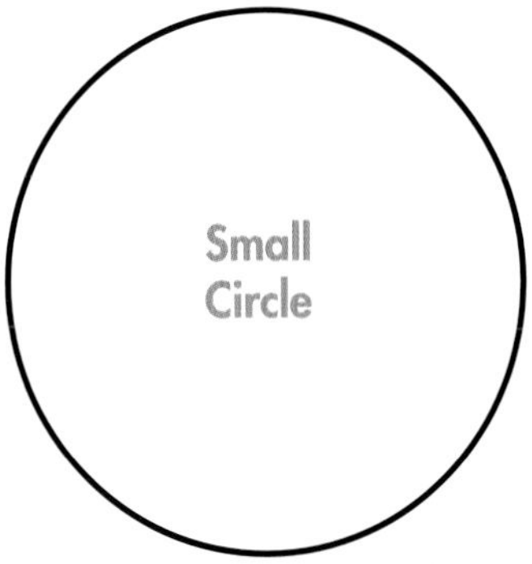

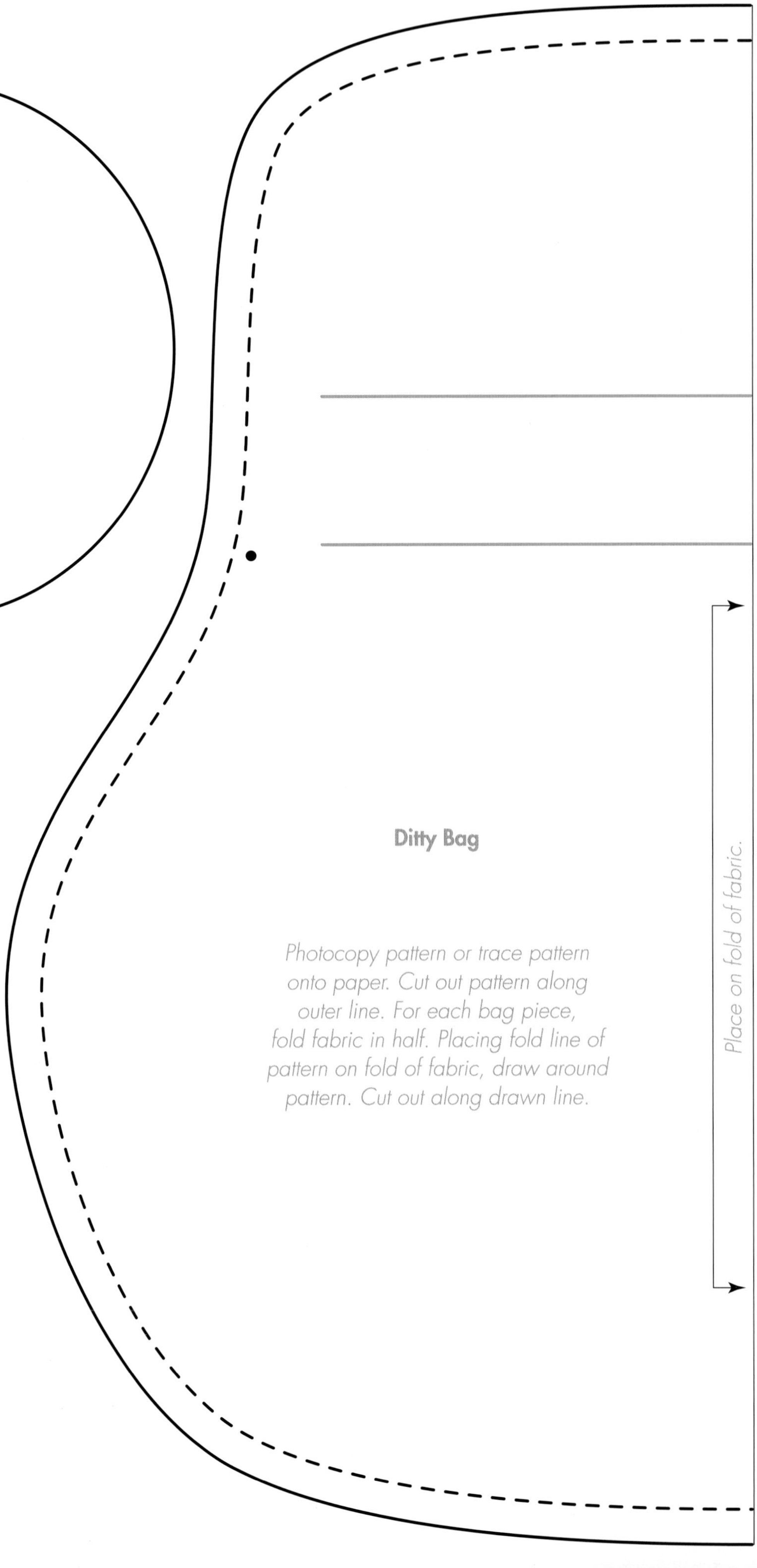

*Photocopy pattern or trace pattern
onto paper. Cut out pattern along
outer line. For each bag piece,
fold fabric in half. Placing fold line of
pattern on fold of fabric, draw around
pattern. Cut out along drawn line.*

Place on fold of fabric.

**Small
Circle**

SHOWER IN Style

I love a pretty bathroom; it makes me feel like I'm at the spa. And since there's no backing on this shower curtain this is a really quick project...so nice!

Tips:

♦ Often, when fabric is printed, the design is repeated at a consistent distance along the length of the fabric. If the project is made of multiple strips you will want the repeats in the fabric to match from piece to piece.

♦ Measure your shower opening to see if a 72" x 80" shower curtain will work.

♦ If you need more length, calculate how much and add that amount when cutting. For example, if you need a 90" long curtain, buy 20" more fabric and cut each panel 10" longer.

♦ Need more width? If it's just a few inches, add 1" to each panel and accent strip. That would be 5" more. If you need more than 5", add to the width of the two accent strips.

♦ Ribbon is a GREAT way to hang your shower curtain. Follow Steps 4-6, page 34. Or you can make fabric tabs. Follow Steps 7-10, page 34.

♦ Spark up your bathroom towels by sewing a strip of fabric to match your shower curtain along the bottom edge. Make a valance to match for the bathroom window (see page 37). Buy a rug in the same colors, pretty soaps, and you are good to go!

Supplies

Yardage is based on 43"/44" (109 cm/112 cm) wide fabric.

5⅛ yds (4.7 m) of shower curtain fabric
2⅝ yds (2.4 m) of accent fabric
2¾ yds (2.5 m) of ¾" (19 mm) wide ribbon **or**
 ¼ yd (23 cm) of fabric for hanging tabs
2⅜ yds (2.2 m) of 13 mm pom-pom trim (optional)
Pinking shears - these are shears that cut a sawtooth edge

Cutting Out The Pieces

All measurements include ¼" seam allowances.
From shower curtain fabric:

♦ To cut 1 piece, make a snip in one selvage edge of the shower curtain fabric about 1" from one cut end. Tear the fabric from selvage to selvage to find the straight of grain. Along the selvage edge, measure 82", snip, and tear in the same manner (**Fig. 1**). This is especially important for a fabric with a repeated design like used here.

Fig. 1

♦ Lay the first piece next to the remaining fabric. Find where the repeats align (**Fig. 2**). Tear a second 82" long piece at the same places on the repeats as the first.

Fig. 2

♦ Using 1 piece, cut 1 **panel** 21" wide x 82" long.
♦ Cut remaining piece in half lengthwise to make 2 **panels** approximately 22" wide x 82" long.

From accent fabric:

♦ Cut 2 *lengthwise* **accent strips** 5½" x 82".

From ribbon or hanging tab fabric:

♦ Cut 11 pieces of **ribbon** 8" long **or** 3 **strips** 2" wide x width of the fabric.

Making The Shower Curtain

Match right sides and raw edges and use a ¼" seam allowance throughout. Refer to Pressing, page 51.

1. Sew the **panels** and **accent strips** together with the narrower panel in the center.
2. Trim the seam allowances with pinking shears so they don't fray.
3. For hems, press all edges ½" to wrong side; press ½" to wrong side again. Topstitch hems in place along inner folded edges.
4. **For ribbon tabs**, fold 1 **ribbon** in half and position it on back of curtain about ½" from one side on top edge of shower curtain; pin. (**Note:** *Fold 1 ribbon in half and place it over your shower curtain rod to see if it is a good length for your rod.*) Repeat with 1 ribbon on opposite end of shower curtain.
5. Evenly space 9 more ribbon tabs on top edge of shower curtain; pin. For a 72" wide shower curtain, that is approximately every 6¼".
6. Refer to **Fig. 3** to topstitch in a "square" to secure each tab.

Fig. 3

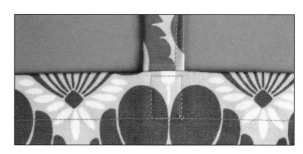

7. **For fabric tabs**, press each long edge of each **strip** ¼" to wrong side.
8. Press each strip in half lengthwise and edgestitch along folded edges.
9. From fabric strips, cut 11 hanging tabs 8" long. (**Note:** *Cut 1 hanging tab, fold it in half, and place it over your shower curtain rod to see if it is a good length for your rod.*)
10. Refer to **Steps 4-6** to attach fabric tabs.
11. Adding trim like the pom-poms (shown on page 36)? Cut pom-pom trim the width of the shower curtain, plus 2". Wrapping the ends of the trim 1" to the back of the shower curtain, pin the trim ¾" below the top edge.
12. Stitch along the top and bottom edge of the lip of the trim.

VALANCE Love

I make LOTS of valances. There are so many great fabrics and it's easy to whip up new valances to change the look of a room. In my living room, the walls are painted chocolate brown and the woodwork is white. The valance allows the woodwork to still be seen and makes for a nice topper.

Curtain Rod Options

The first thing you need to do is buy a curtain rod to fit your window. There are many curtain rod options available today. The following are the most common:

♦ Tension rod that fits inside your window casing.
♦ Curtain rod with a return that wraps around the edges of the window frame and mounts to the wall.
♦ Decorative curtain rod that is mounted to the wall with brackets and extends out from the wall.

Supplies

Note: Additional yardage may be required if valance is wider than 80" or longer than 9".

¼ yd (23 cm) of top fabric for valance narrower than 38" (97 cm) or ½ yd (46 cm) of top fabric for valance 38"- 80" (97 cm - 203 cm) wide

¼ yd (23 cm) of bottom fabric for valance narrower than 38" (97 cm) or ½ yd (46 cm) of bottom fabric for valance 38"- 80" (97 cm - 203 cm) wide

How To Measure For A Valance

Follow the manufacturer's instructions to mount your curtain rod.

The instructions given here are for a flat valance that is 9" long when finished. I suggest you cut some paper the width and length you think you'd like. Tape this up on the curtain rod with blue painters tape. Step back and see what you think about the length and width before cutting your fabric.

It's decision time! Here are a few things to think about:

♦ Decide if you want a fairly "flat" look or if you want the valance to be "fuller." Measure the length of the curtain rod you wish to cover. For a fuller valance, add 5" to 15" inches to the width, depending on the fullness desired. A valance that covers the returns of the rod or that is fuller will require a wider valance.

♦ Decide if you want a longer valance. If you do, add the desired number of inches to the length of the bottom fabric.

Cutting Out The Pieces

All measurements include ¼" seam allowances.

If your paper valance (page 38) is 38" or narrower, one crosswise strip of fabric will be wide enough for your valance. If your measurement is wider than 38", multiple crosswise strips will be required.

Often, when fabric is printed the design is repeated at a consistent distance along the length of the fabric. If the valance is made of multiple strips you will want the repeats in the fabric to match from piece to piece.

From Each Fabric:

♦ **If paper valance is narrower than 38"**, cut 1 *crosswise* **strip** 8" x desired width plus 2" for side hems.

♦ **If paper valance is 38" – 80" wide and your fabric does not have a repeat**, cut as many 8" long *crosswise* **strips** as needed to equal width of valance plus 2½" for seam allowances and side hems.

♦ **If paper valance is 38" – 80" wide and your fabric has a repeat**, you will need 8" long crosswide strips to equal desired width plus 2½" for seam allowances and side hems.

To cut first strip, make a snip in one selvage edge of the fabric about 1" from one cut end. Tear the fabric from selvage to selvage to find the straight of grain. Along the selvage edge, measure 8", snip, and tear in the same manner.

Lay the first piece next to the remaining fabric. Find where the repeats align. Tear a second strip at the same places on the repeats as the first.

Making The Valance

*Instructions are written for a valance narrower than 38". If a wider valance is desired, match repeats and sew strips together along short ends before beginning. Match right sides and raw edges and use a ¼" seam allowance throughout. Refer to **Pressing**, page 51.*

1. Sew the top and bottom fabric **strips** together along one long edge.

2. Press the seam allowance toward the **top** fabric. It will be covered when making the casing.

3. For hems, press all edges ½" to wrong side. Press sides and bottom edge ½" to the wrong side again. Do not press under **top** again.

4. Topstitch side and bottom hems in place along inner folded edges.

5. With the wrong side facing up, place the valance on the ironing board. Fold the top down so it covers the seam allowance and is about ⅛" over the seamline.

6. Using steam, press the folded edge so there is a nice crease.

7. Turn valance to the **front** and pin the casing along the seam (**Fig. 1**) in the bottom fabric.

Fig. 1

8. Sewing from **front** of valance, topstitch as close to the seam as possible on the bottom fabric to secure the casing (**Fig. 2**).

Fig. 2

Embellish for fun! Sew pom-poms, ribbon or trim over the seam.

This is the perfect summer spread for the bed! Bring loads of color into your room by selecting 8 fabrics. These fabrics will blend and swirl into each other when made up to create a delightful bed cover.

Finished Size:
90" x 90" (229 cm x 229 cm)

Finished Block Size:
30" x 30" (76 cm x 76 cm)

Tips:

♦ If you are using a thin or light-color fabric, audition your backing behind it. Place both fabrics wrong sides together. Lay the fabrics on the bed. Can you see the backing fabric through the top fabric? If you can, then just add a layer of muslin or flannel between the two layers when sewing.

♦ If you want a firmer spread, use a layer of flannel or muslin between the top and backing.

♦ For a super simple spread, don't add a backing. Just hem all 4 sides and spread it on the bed!

Supplies

Yardage is based on 43"/44" (109 cm/112 cm) wide fabric.

⅝ yd (57 cm) of stripe fabric
⅝ yd (57 cm) of light green small print fabric
2 yds (1.8 m) of light green floral print fabric
2⅝ yds (2.4 m) of blue large floral print fabric
1⅜ yds (1.3 m) of tan floral print fabric #1
1⅜ yds (1.3 m) of tan floral print fabric #2
1⅜ yds (1.3 m) of tan floral print fabric #3
1 yd (91 cm) of tan floral print fabric #4
7⅞ yds (7.2 m) of backing fabric

Cutting Out The Pieces

All measurements include ¼" seam allowances.
From stripe fabric:
♦ Cut 18 **small squares** 5½" x 5½".
From light green small print fabric:
♦ Cut 18 **small squares** 5½" x 5½".
From light green floral print fabric:
♦ Cut 8 **rectangles** 10½" x 20½".

From blue large floral print fabric:
♦ Cut 10 **rectangles** 10½" x 20½".
From tan floral print fabric #1:
♦ Cut 5 **rectangles** 10½" x 20½".
From tan floral print fabric #2:
♦ Cut 10 **large squares** 10½" x 10½".
From tan floral print fabric #3:
♦ Cut 4 **rectangles** 10½" x 20½".
From tan floral print fabric #4:
♦ Cut 8 **large squares** 10½" x 10½".

Making The Spread

*Refer to **Spread Top Diagram**, page 43. Match right sides and raw edges and use a ¼" seam allowance throughout. Refer to **Pressing**, page 51.*

1. Sew one stripe **small square** to one light green **small square** to make **Unit 1**. Press seam allowances to the stripe fabric. Make 18 Unit 1's.

Unit 1 (make 18)

2. Rotating Units, sew 2 Unit 1's together to make 4-Patch Unit. Make 9 4-Patch Units.

4-Patch Unit (make 9)

40

Pat Sloan's "I Can't Believe I'm Sewing!"

3. Sew 2 blue large floral print **rectangles** and 1 tan floral print #1 **rectangle** together along long edges to make Unit 2. Make 5 Unit 2's.

Unit 2 (make 5)

4. Sew 2 tan floral print #2 **large squares** and 1 4-Patch Unit together to make Unit 3. Make 5 Unit 3's.

Unit 3 (make 5)

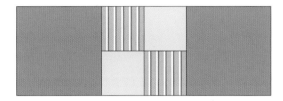

5. Sew 1 Unit 2 to 1 Unit 3 to make Block 1. Make 5 Block 1's.

Block 1 (make 5)

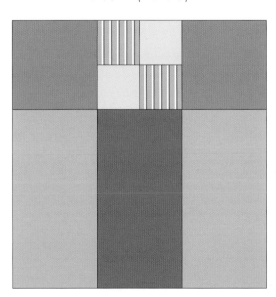

6. Sew 2 light green floral print **rectangles** to 1 tan floral print #3 **rectangle** to make Unit 4. Make 4 Unit 4's.

Unit 4 (make 4)

7. Sew 2 tan floral print #4 **large squares** and 1 4-Patch Unit together to make Unit 5. Make 4 Unit 5's.

Unit 5 (make 4)

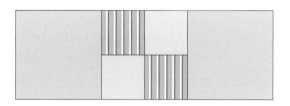

8. Sew 1 Unit 4 to 1 Unit 5 to make Block 2. Make 4 Block 2's.

Block 2 (make 4)

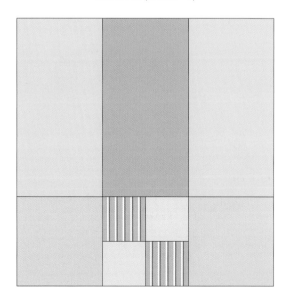

9. Sew 2 Block 1's and 1 Block 2 together to make **Row A**. Make 2 Row A's.

10. Sew 2 Block 2's and 1 Block 1 together to make **Row B**.

11. Sew Row A's and Row B together to make Spread Top.

Finishing Your Spread

1. Refer to **Preparing The Backing**, page 52, to piece and trim backing fabrics to make a square 94" x 94"; press.

Tip: Your community center or church should have tables you can use for pinning. It's nice to be able to lay the piece out flat for this step.

2. Lay backing, right side up, on as big a table as you can find. Clamp 2 sides to the table so the backing is flat.

3. Center top, right side down, on the backing. **Note:** If adding a layer of flannel or muslin, center flannel or muslin on wrong side of spread top.

4. Using safety pins, pin the two layers together 1" from the edge all the way around. (This allows you room to sew without removing the pins.) Place 2 or 3 pins in the center area so the fabrics won't shift and it will be easier to handle. When you have pinned all the edges you can, unclamp and shift the whole thing to pin the rest.

5. Leaving about a 10" opening for turning, sew all sides together. Trim backing even with top. Remove the safety pins and turn the spread right side out, being sure to push out the corners. Press well so the edges are flat.

6. To close the opening and make a nice edge, edgestitch around the outside of the spread close to the edge.

7. Stitch "in the ditch" along the 2 long vertical seamlines. This will hold the layers together nicely. *Note: If you added a muslin or flannel layer in the middle, it will be good to secure all 3 together.*

Put your new spread on your bed and enjoy!!! Maybe make a few adorable pillows to go with it!

Spread Top Diagram

"ROUND AND ROUND WE GO" PILLOWS

These pillows are a fabulous way to use up scraps from bigger projects. Cut 2½" strips from your "leftovers" and throw them in a bag. When you need a pillow, dump out your strips. Sort them into appealing color combos, make a few pillows, and you have gifts, updated decor, and accents galore!

Finished Size:
16" x 16" (41 cm x 41 cm)

Supplies
Yardage is based on 43"/44" (109 cm/112 cm) wide fabric and will make 1 pillow.
   Assorted scrap fabrics for pillow top
   ⅜ yd (34 cm) of backing fabric*
   16" x 16" (41 cm x 41 cm) pillow form

*I used cotton fabric like the front, but you could back your pillow with denim or even fleece if you want the back to be very soft. You may have leftovers of those too!

Cutting Out The Pieces
All measurements include ¼" seam allowances.
From the assorted scraps for pillow top:
   ♦ Refer to **Cutting Diagram** to cut **center** and **strips** for the pillow top.
From backing fabric:
   ♦ Cut 2 **rectangles** 10½" x 16½".

Making The Pillow
Match right sides and raw edges and use a ¼" seam allowance throughout. You will be sewing **clockwise** *around the pillow. Refer to* **Pressing**, *page 51.*

1. Sew pieces **1** and **2** to each other; press seam allowances open.
2. Sew piece **3** to pieces 1-2.
3. Sew piece **4** to pieces 1-2-3.
4. Repeat in this manner until you have sewn all 13 pieces together to make pillow top 16½" x 16½".
5. Press 1 long edge ¼" to wrong side on each backing **rectangle**; press ¼" to wrong side again. Topstitch folded edges in place.
6. Overlapping topstitched edges of pillow backs to make a 16½" x 16½" square, sew pillow backs to pillow top. Turn pillow right side out; press.
7. Insert the pillow form.

Cutting Diagram

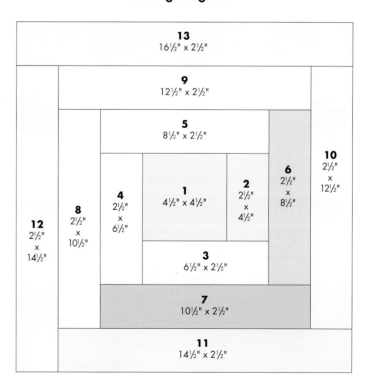

"EASY PEASY" Pillowcases

Custom pillowcases are so special and make your room look like a decorator just left! With a bit of fabric you can match any spread you have on your bed. You can use solid fabric or the prints you used for your spread to pull the whole look together.

Supplies

Yardage is based on 43"/44" (109 cm/112 cm) wide fabric and will make 2 pillowcases.

- 1⅝ yds (1.5 m) of fabric #1 for body of pillowcase
- ⅝ yd (57 cm) of fabric #2 for trim

Cutting Out The Pieces

All measurements include ¼" seam allowances.

From fabric #1:
- ♦ Cut 2 **rectangles** 26" x width of fabric.

From fabric #2:
- ♦ Cut 2 **rectangles** 10" x width of fabric.

Making The Pillowcases

*Match right sides and raw edges and use a ¼" seam allowance throughout. Refer to **Pressing**, page 51.*

1. Sew 1 fabric #2 **rectangle** to 1 fabric #1 **rectangle** along one long edge. Press the seam allowance towards fabric #2 rectangle.

2. Matching short edges, fold the piece in half so you have a piece that now looks like a pillowcase with a very long end; pin.

3. Sew along the long side and the fabric #1 short edge. Do **not** turn pillowcase right side out at this time.

Tip: To keep the seam allowances from creating a lot of threads when you wash the pillowcase, use pinking shears to trim them.

4. Press the open edge of the pillowcase ½" to the wrong side. Fold the pressed edge to the wrong side again so it is covering the sewn seam. The sewn seam will be hidden under the pressed edge. Press the fold line well…steam is good. You want a nice crease.

5. Turn the pillowcase right side out.

6. Checking that the folded edge is covering all the seam allowance, pin the folded edge in place from the **OUTSIDE**.

7. Sew around the pillowcase as close to the seam as possible, on the fabric #1 piece, catching the folded edge of the pillowcase and encasing the seam allowance so the pillowcase is very "finished".

Insert your pillow and take a little nap…good job!

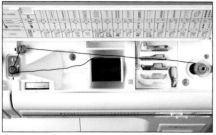
Fig. 1a

Fig. 1b

Fig. 2

Fig. 3

Fig. 4

PREPARING YOUR Machine

Winding Bobbins

Your goal when winding a bobbin is to have the thread feed evenly onto the bobbin with an even tension on the thread. On most machines this is pretty easy to do. Refer to your sewing machine manual for the bobbin winding procedure specific to your machine. But if you don't have a manual and are not sure what to do, here are a few general instructions:

♦ To wind the bobbin, put the thread on the spool pin and put the cap on the pin. Although machines vary in their placement, now the thread has to go through a series of thread guides or may even by threaded in the needle before winding around the bobbin (**Figs. 1a & 1b**). This makes the bobbin winding consistent and taut. Look for markings on the machine body. Many have little arrows to show you where the thread needs to go (**Fig. 2**).

♦ There will be a short bobbin winder spindle somewhere on the top right or bottom right of the machine. There should be a bobbin winder stop next to it. If your bobbin has a hole (or holes), place the thread end through a hole in the bobbin. Pull a few inches of thread through. Put the bobbin onto the spindle and push the stop next to it (**Fig. 3**).

♦ If your bobbin does not have holes, place the bobbin onto the spindle and push the stop next to it. Wrap the thread around the bobbin several times.

♦ Hold onto the thread end and push the foot control. If the needle goes up and down, this means you have to disengage the hand wheel (**Fig. 4**). This will not be required for all machines.

♦ Holding onto the thread end until it breaks away, push the foot control to wind the bobbin until full. Your machine should stop when the bobbin winder stop knows the bobbin has enough thread.

♦ Cut excess thread from the hole in the bobbin and the thread that runs from the bobbin to the spool.

Pat Sloan's "I Can't Believe I'm Sewing!"

Inserting The Bobbin

The bobbin is inserted in one of two ways depending on how the machine is made. It can be inserted in a bobbin case on the top of the machine's bed or into a bobbin case behind a small door in the front or end of the machine's bed.

Top Drop-In

♦ Raise the presser foot. Pull about 4" of thread from the bobbin. Making sure the thread is winding off the bobbin in a counterclockwise direction, insert the bobbin into the case as shown (**Fig. 5**).

♦ Guide the thread into the notch of the bobbin case (**Fig. 5**) and position the thread towards the back of the machine. Close the slide plate or replace the cover, allowing the thread to extend through the slot between the slide plate and needle plate.

♦ Holding the end of the top thread and using your hand wheel, turn the needle down into the well and back up. The bobbin thread will "loop up" with the top thread (**Fig. 6**). Pull the bobbin thread to the top above the throat plate.

Fig. 5

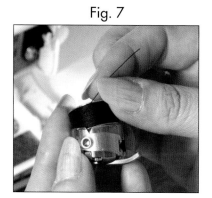

Fig. 6

Fig. 7

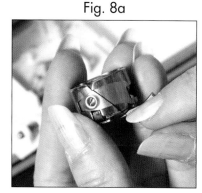

Fig. 8a

Fig. 8b

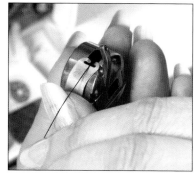

Fig. 9

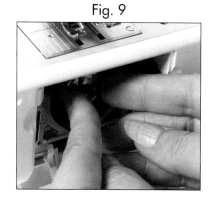

Front Load

♦ Raise the presser foot. Open the bobbin door and lift the hinged latch to pull the bobbin case out of the machine. Remove the bobbin from the bobbin case by releasing the hinged latch and letting the bobbin fall out.

♦ Hold the bobbin case with one hand. Insert the bobbin with the thread running in a clockwise direction (**Fig. 7**).

♦ Pull the thread through the slit and under the finger (**Figs. 8a & 8b**). The thread should advance with little resistance when you pull it.

♦ Hold the bobbin case by the hinged latch (**Fig. 9**). Insert the bobbin case into the housing.

♦ Holding the end of the top thread and using your hand wheel, turn the needle down into the well and back up. The bobbin thread will "loop up" with the top thread (**Fig. 6**). Pull the bobbin thread to the top above the throat plate.

Fig. 10

Needle Clamp Screw

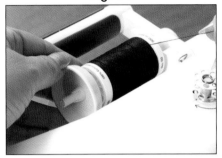

Fig. 11

Fig. 12

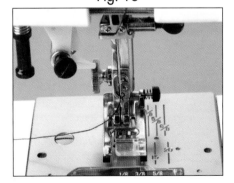

Fig. 13

THreading 101

The Needle

♦ First put in a **NEW NEEDLE**. Yes...it is necessary. Depending on how long ago this machine was used, the needle may be in really bad shape. Get a pack of size 80 or 90 general-purpose needles to start.

♦ Raise the presser foot to its highest position.

♦ Look for a needle clamp screw above the needle (Fig. 10). Loosen the screw and the needle will drop out...so **HOLD ONTO THE NEEDLE**... don't let it drop into the hole in the throat plate.

♦ Insert the new needle. Most needles usually have a flat side. The flat part is inserted facing the back of the machine. Tighten the screw.

Threading The Machine

Many machines have arrows or diagrams on the machine itself to help you with threading. And hopefully you have the manual, which will usually have a diagram that shows you exactly what to do. All machines are a bit different, but the basics are:

♦ Put thread on the spool holder, and put the cap (if applicable) on the end so the thread won't fly off when sewing (Fig. 11).

♦ The thread travels over to the left side of the machine and there is a thread guide(s) to place it through (Fig. 12) for tension control.

♦ Now the thread winds down the front of the machine and back up in the take-up lever. This has a "slit" that the thread slides into from back to front. There is a big hook in the take-up lever that the thread rests on.

♦ At this point the thread is now down near the needle. There may be a tension "loop" to put the thread under before you thread the needle.

♦ Thread the needle (Fig. 13). Most machines thread from front to back but some machines thread left to right.

CLEANING & OILING your Machine

Fig. 1

Fig. 2a

A sewing machine is like a car — you have to do some maintenance on it occasionally or one day it will just stop working. Luckily no gas is required!

Read your manual to determine if and when your machine requires oiling. Some machines are "oil impregnated" and do not require oiling.

Cleaning your machine is the first step because you need to be sure there isn't a pile of lint inside. The manual will give you the basic cleaning instructions for your machine. Here are things you need to do if you don't have a manual:

♦ Slide the throat plate open or remove it and clean out all the lint with a soft paintbrush or pipe cleaner. This area will need cleaning after each project or two that you do. That lint build up might get in the way of your stitches and cause bad sewing... not good!

Fig. 2b

♦ Find where the bobbin is loaded. It might be right below the throat plate, it might be on the lower front (open the little door), or it might be on the left "end" of the machine. Remove the bobbin and bobbin case (Fig. 1). Clean out any lint with a paintbrush or pipe cleaner (Fig. 2a & 2b).

Fig. 3

♦ If your machine requires oiling, use sewing machine oil to place a few drops of oil in the bobbin case housing (Fig. 3). If you don't have new oil, get some at a fabric or sewing machine store.

♦ Put the bobbin case, bobbin and throat plate back in place. Sew on a scrap of fabric to absorb any excess oil.

♦ Clean any lint or grease away from the shaft above the needle. This is the part that goes up into the machine when the needle is all the way up... and it can get dirty and drop stuff onto your project. You don't want that to happen!

ROTARY Cutting

All of the fabric pieces for the projects in this leaflet can be cut using scissors but if you're going to really **GET GOING** and **CRANK** out lots of projects, you are going to want to learn to use a rotary cutter. Most of the projects have straight edges and that's where a rotary cutter will **SPEED** you along!

In order to rotary cut you will need a rotary cutter, an 18" x 24" (or larger) cutting mat, and a 6" x 24" acrylic rotary cutting ruler. While these may be a bit of an investment in the beginning, they are worth every penny you pay! They will make your life so much easier.

Fig. 1

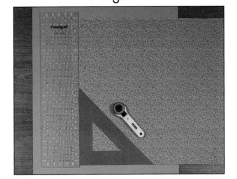

Fig. 2

Fig. 3

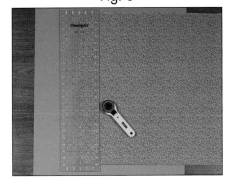

1. Before cutting needed pieces, you will need to straighten 1 cut edge of your fabric. Place fabric on the cutting mat, with the selvage edges together and the fold of the fabric toward you. To straighten the uneven fabric edge, make the first "squaring up" cut by placing the right edge of your 24" ruler over the left raw edge of the fabric. Place a triangle or square ruler, with the lower edge carefully aligned with the folded edge of the fabric against the right edge of your 24" ruler (Fig. 1). Holding the ruler firmly with your left hand, place your little finger off the left edge to anchor the ruler; remove the triangle or ruler. Using a smooth downward motion, make a cut by running the blade of the rotary cutter firmly along the right edge of the ruler (Fig. 2). **Always** cut in a direction **away** from your body.

2. When cutting pieces, first you will cut a strip as wide as 1 side of the square or rectangle called for in your project instructions. All strips are cut from the selvage-to-selvage width of the fabric unless otherwise indicated in project instructions. To cut each of the strips required for a project, place the ruler over the cut edge of the fabric, aligning desired marking on the ruler with the cut edge (Fig. 3); make the cut. When cutting several strips from a single piece of fabric, it may be necessary to occasionally re-square the edge as shown in **Step 1**.

3. To square up selvage ends of a strip before cutting pieces, place folded strip on mat with selvage ends to your right. Aligning a horizontal marking on ruler with 1 long edge of strip, use rotary cutter to trim selvage to make end of strip square and even (Fig. 4). Turn strip (or entire mat) so that cut end is to your left before making subsequent cuts.

4. Pieces such as squares or rectangles can now be cut from strips. Usually strips remain folded, and pieces are cut in pairs after ends of strips are squared up. To cut squares or rectangles from a strip, place ruler over left end of strip, aligning desired marking on ruler with cut end of strip. To ensure perfectly square cuts, align a horizontal marking on ruler with 1 long edge of strip (Fig. 5) before making a cut.

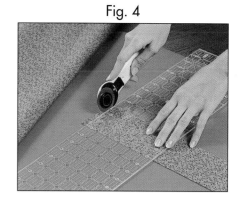

Fig. 4

Fig. 5

PRESSING

♦ Use steam iron set on "Cotton" for all pressing.

♦ Press after sewing each seam.

♦ Seam allowances are almost always pressed to one side, usually toward darker fabric. However, to reduce bulk it may occasionally be necessary to press seam allowances toward the lighter fabric or even to press them open.

♦ To prevent dark fabric seam allowance from showing through light fabric, trim darker seam allowance slightly narrower than lighter seam allowance.

♦ To press long seams without curving or other distortion, lay strips across width of the ironing board.

Pat Sloan's "I Can't Believe I'm Sewing!"

QuiLTING

Quilting holds the layers of the quilt together and can be done by hand or machine. Because marking, layering, and quilting are interrelated and may be done in different orders depending on circumstances, please read entire **Quilting** section, pages 52 – 53.

Preparing The Backing

To allow for slight shifting of the quilt top during quilting, the backing should be approximately 2" larger on all sides than the quilt top. Yardage requirements given for quilt backings are calculated for 43"/44" wide fabric. To piece backing, use the following instructions:

1. Cut backing fabric into three lengths slightly longer than measurement given in project instructions. Trim selvages. Sew long edges together to form a single piece.
2. Trim backing to correct size and press seam allowances open.

Types OF QuiLTING

In the Ditch Quilting

Quilting along seamlines is called "in the ditch" quilting. This type of quilting should be done on side **opposite** seam allowance and does not have to be marked.

Outline Quilting

Quilting a consistent distance, usually ¼", from seam is called "outline" quilting. Outline quilting may be marked, or ¼" masking tape may be placed along seamlines for quilting guide. (Do not leave tape on quilt longer than necessary, since it may leave an adhesive residue.)

Pat Sloan's "I Can't Believe I'm Sewing!"

Marking Quilting Lines

Quilting lines may be marked using fabric marking pencils, chalk markers, water- or air-soluble pens, or lead pencils.

Simple quilting designs may be marked with chalk or chalk pencil after basting. A small area may be marked, and then quilted, before moving to next area to be marked. Intricate designs should be marked before basting using a more durable marker.

Caution: Pressing may permanently set some marks. Test different markers on scrap fabric to find one that marks clearly and can be thoroughly removed.

A wide variety of pre-cut quilting stencils, as well as entire books of quilting patterns, are available. Using a stencil makes it easier to mark intricate or repetitive designs.

To make a stencil from a pattern, center template plastic over pattern and use a permanent marker to trace pattern onto plastic. Use a craft knife with single or double blade to cut channels along traced lines (Fig. 1).

Fig. 1

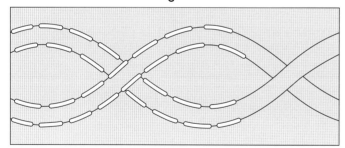

Choosing The Batting

The appropriate batting will make quilting easier. For fine hand quilting, choose low-loft batting. Types of batting include cotton, polyester, wool, cotton/wool blend, cotton/polyester blend, and silk.

When selecting batting, refer to package labels for characteristics and care instructions. Cut batting same size as prepared backing.

Machine Quilting Methods

Use general-purpose thread in bobbin. Do not use quilting thread. Thread the needle of machine with general-purpose thread or transparent monofilament thread to make quilting blend with quilt top fabrics. Use decorative thread, such as a metallic or contrasting-color general-purpose thread, to make quilting lines stand out more.

Straight-Line Quilting

The following instructions are for straight-line quilting, which requires a walking foot or even-feed foot. The term "straight-line" is somewhat deceptive, since curves (especially gentle ones) as well as straight lines can be stitched with this technique.

1. Using the same color general-purpose thread in the needle and bobbin avoids "dots" of bobbin thread being pulled to the surface.
2. Using general-purpose thread, which matches the backing in the bobbin, will add pattern and dimension to the quilt without adding contrasting color. Refer to your owner's manual for recommended tension settings.
3. Set stitch length for 6 to 10 stitches per inch and attach the walking foot to sewing machine.
4. After pin-basting, decide which section of the quilt will have the longest continuous quilting line, oftentimes the area from center top to center bottom. Leaving the area exposed where you will place your first line of quilting, roll up each edge of the quilt to help reduce the bulk, keeping fabrics smooth. Smaller projects may not need to be rolled.
5. Start stitching at beginning of longest quilting line, using very short stitches for the first ¼" to "lock" quilting. Stitch across project, using one hand on each side of walking foot to slightly spread fabric and to guide fabric through machine. Lock stitches at end of quilting line.
6. Continue machine quilting, stitching longer quilting lines first to stabilize quilt before moving on to other areas.

CREATE A SEWING IDEA Notebook

As you are out and about things will inspire you or you'll see ideas you want to try out. The thing to do is create a notebook of these ideas that you can look through. Use a simple 3-ring binder, cover it with **COOL** fabric if you like, then start filling it with the following:

♦ Photos you take of items or colors you love. Take your digital camera with you and snap away at all things you love. Create a collage of the photos and print it off for your notebook.
♦ Magazine pages - just put them in plastic sleeves.
♦ Snips of fabric and trim you have that you want to use. Staple those to a sheet of paper and put in the notebook.
♦ Advertisements that catch your eye for color combinations.

GLOSSARY

Backstitch – A stitch in reverse done at the beginning and end of seams to lock the stitch in place.

Backstitch Button – The button on your machine that makes your machine stitch backwards or backstitch.

Basting – Using large, loose stitches to temporarily join layers of fabric together. Basting can be done by hand or by machine.

Batting – The fiber used as the filler between two pieces of fabric to form a quilt or to give a project body. It can be cotton, polyester, cotton/polyester blend, wool, or silk.

Bias – the direction along the 45° angle on the fabric. It has the most stretch.

Bobbin – The part of the sewing machine that holds the lower thread.

Bobbin Case – The part of the sewing machine that holds the bobbin.

Bobbin Winder Spindle – The part of the sewing machine where the bobbin is placed when filling a bobbin.

Bobbin Winder Stop – The part of the sewing machine next to the bobbin winder spindle that automatically stops the winding of the bobbin when the bobbin is full.

Crosswise Grain – The fabric grain that runs perpendicular to the selvages. It has a little more stretch than the lengthwise grain.

Edgestitch – A line of decorative straight stitches that are stitched along the edge of a fabric piece, such as around a pocket.

Fabric Grain – The lengthwise and crosswise threads in woven fabric are the grain.

Feed Dogs – The saw-tooth edge machine part under the throat plate that moves the fabric beneath the presser foot.

Foot Control – The part of the sewing machine that is placed on the floor and controls the sewing speed by pressing the control with your foot.

Grain Line Arrow – A line printed on a pattern with arrows on each end that indicates the proper way to align the pattern on the grain of the fabric.

Hand Wheel – A knob or button on the end of the sewing machine used to disengage the needle shaft and prevent it from going up and down.

Lengthwise Grain – The fabric grain that runs parallel to the selvages. Fabrics are most stable and have the least stretch on the lengthwise grain.

Machine Bed – The flat work surface surrounding the needle plate area of the machine.

Needle Clamp Screw – A small thumbscrew above the needle that when tightened, holds the needle in place.

Needle Down – A feature on some machines that allows the machine to automatically stop sewing with the needle in the fabric. This keeps your fabric from slipping and creating a crooked stitching line.

Needle Plate – The flat, metal work area around the needle area of the machine; it has a hole or slot that the needle passes through when sewing.

Needle Threader – An especially nice feature on some machines that helps you to thread the needle.

Oil Impregnated – Some machines are permanently treated with oil and do not require additional oiling.

Presser Foot – The part of the sewing machine that holds the fabric flat against the throat plate when stitching. There are a variety of presser foot types available for most machines.

Presser Foot Lever – A lever on the sewing machine used to raise and lower the presser foot.

Quilting – The stitching that holds the three layers (top, batting, and backing) of the quilt together. Can be done by hand or machine.

Rotary Cutter – A fabric cutting tool with a circular blade that cuts through several layers of fabric at once.

Rotary Cutting Mat – A mat used to protect the work surface and preserve the blade's sharpness when using a rotary cutter.

Rotary Cutting Ruler – A thick, clear plastic ruler used as a cutting guide when using a rotary cutter. Available in a variety of sizes and shapes.

Seam Allowance – The area from your stitching line to the edge of the fabric. Garment construction usually uses a $5/8$" seam allowance, sewing home décor usually uses a $1/2$" seam allowance, and quilt piecing usually uses a $1/4$" seam allowance.

Seam Allowance Guide – The area to the right of the needle marked in $1/8$" increments; used for guiding the machine to obtain an even width seam allowance.

Seam Line – The straight or curved line on which the stitches are formed.

Seam Ripper – A sharp, curved-tip tool used to lift and cut when removing stitches.

Selvage – The lengthwise finished edges of the fabric.

Sewing Idea Notebook – A notebook used to store photos, magazine pages, fabric and trim samples, or any other items that inspire you.

Sewing Machine Manual – A booklet that comes with your machine that gives you instructions specific to the operation of your machine.

Slide Plate – The plastic or metal cover placed over the bobbin case.

Spool Pin – The spindle that holds the thread on the top of the sewing machine.

Stitch Length – The average stitch length is 2.5 to 3 mm or approximately 12 stitches per inch.

Stitch Length Regulator – The device on your machine that allows you to set the length of the stitch.

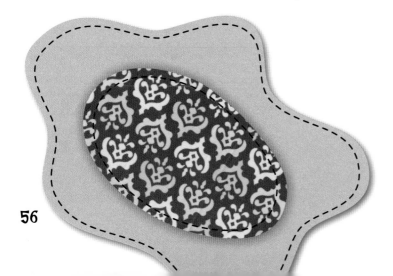

Stitch Width Regulator – The device on your machine that allows you to set the width of the stitch.

Straight Stitch – The basic stitch of all sewing machines; a straight line of stitches.

Supply List – The part of the project instructions that tell you the supplies you will need to complete the project.

Take-up Lever – The part of the sewing machine that holds the needle thread and pulls it up as the stitch is being made.

Thread Tension Control – Used to adjust the tension on the top thread so that you have beautiful stitches.

Thread/Tension Guides – A series of knobs, slots, or loops through which the thread passes from the spool to the needle. These guides control the amount of tension that is placed on the thread and help to create an attractive stitch.

Throat Plate – The removable plate on the machine bed that covers the bobbin and has an opening for the feed dogs and needle.

Topstitch – A line of decorative straight stitches that are stitched a consistent distance, such as ¼" from the edge of a fabric piece, such as around a pocket.

Walking Foot – A sewing machine presser foot that moves the top fabric through the machine at the same rate as the feed dogs move the bottom fabric. Used when sewing extra thick fabrics and for machine quilting.

Zigzag Stitch – A side-to-side machine stitch. The width and length of the stitch can be adjusted.

Metric Conversion Chart

Inches x 2.54 = centimeters (cm)	Yards x .9144 = meters (m)
Inches x 25.4 = millimeters (mm)	Yards x 91.44 = centimeters (cm)
Inches x .0254 = meters (m)	Centimeters x .3937 = inches (")
	Meters x 1.0936 = yards (yd)

Standard Equivalents

⅛"	3.2 mm	0.32 cm	⅛ yard	11.43 cm	0.11 m
¼"	6.35 mm	0.635 cm	¼ yard	22.86 cm	0.23 m
⅜"	9.5 mm	0.95 cm	⅜ yard	34.29 cm	0.34 m
½"	12.7 mm	1.27 cm	½ yard	45.72 cm	0.46 m
⅝"	15.9 mm	1.59 cm	⅝ yard	57.15 cm	0.57 m
¾"	19.1 mm	1.91 cm	¾ yard	68.58 cm	0.69 m
⅞"	22.2 mm	2.22 cm	⅞ yard	80 cm	0.8 m
1 "	25.4 mm	2.54 cm	1 yard	91.44 cm	0.91 m

MEET Pat SLoaN

Pat Sloan's knowledge of sewing is impressive.
She started with doll clothes when she was a little girl and went on to make her own clothing, which she did for many years. Her continuing love of the skill shines through as she breaks down the learning process for sewing her home fashions and accessories. The result is a fun selection of designs with clear instructions in easy stages—an approachable process, even for folks who've never before cut fabric or threaded a needle.

Allocating her at-home time between drawing patterns and developing fabrics, Pat still finds time to update her Web site. Visitors to QuiltersHome.com can read her blog, subscribe to her newsletter, and check for her quilting workshops in their area. They'll also find a variety of publications, patterns, notions, and Pat's popular fabric lines from P&B Textiles, all available for purchase. There are even a few freebie patterns just for inspiration. And on icantbelieveim.com, Pat's quilt technique classes are available on demand as downloads.

The Virginia resident says, "These days, my life is all about quilting and sewing, twenty-four/seven. I've been fulltime at this career for eight years. My husband does the managing—shipping, ordering, and accounting—keeping me free to teach, lecture, and do the creative side. Our time to just relax happens

Pat Sloan's "I Can't Believe I'm Sewing!"

while we travel for work. Gregg and I drive to most of our workshops and lectures because of all the equipment we bring along. We meet the nicest people! And we get to see lots of new places that are within a day's drive from home."

With their business doing so well, you might think that the Sloans would be ready to just sit back and take it easy now and then. Instead, Gregg and Pat have found a way to take their work with them on vacation. They've recently added quilting cruises to their schedule of events, with Pat teaching up to 50 students between ports of call. And if there's anyone who can take the fun crafts of sewing and quilting and make them downright exhilarating, it's Pat Sloan.

PAT'S THANK YOU'S!

To make the projects, I used Mettler® thread and Mountain Mist batting.

Thank you to Free Spirit Fabrics, P & B Textiles,
Andover Fabrics, and Red Rooster Fabric companies for providing
many of the fabrics used in the projects for this book.

Also, a special thank you to Bernina® of America, Inc.
for providing my sewing machine and to Olfa® for providing
my rotary cutter, rulers, and mat.

PRODUCTION TeaM

Technical Writer – Lisa Lancaster
Editorial Writer – Susan McManus Johnson
Senior Graphic Artist – Lora Puls
Graphic Artist – Amy Temple
Production Artists – Frances Huddleston and Janie Wright
Photographer – Ken West
Photo Stylist – Sondra Daniel

For digital downloads of Leisure Arts' best-selling designs, visit http://www.leisureartslibrary.com.